SUCCESSFUL SUBSTITUTE TEACHING

In the Elementary Classroom

May Gilden

CONTENTS

May Gilden

Visit my author page: amazon.com/author/maygilden

Printed in the United States of America

First Printing: Aug 2019

ISBN- 9781089900184

INTRODUCTION

The Role of the Substitute Teacher

Substitute teachers play a vital role in every school. A good substitute gives teachers peace of mind when they need to be away from their classrooms. A good substitute teacher is someone that the principal can rely on to carry out classroom duties competently. And most importantly, a good substitute teacher provides a calm and stable environment for students so that they feel safe, despite a break in their normal routine.

Career Opportunity

Substitute teaching can be a meaningful career, allowing for flexibility and freedom, while providing a good income and a positive experience. It also provides a great opportunity if you are thinking about pursuing a full- time teaching career because substitute teachers are often considered first when there are staff openings.

Rewards and Challenges

Even though substitute teaching can be a very rewarding experience, it is not always easy. There may be some classes that try your patience and make you wonder if you will be able to survive the school day. Remember that you are human, and that you will have both good days and bad days.

I remember my very first day as a substitute teacher. I was called to an emotional support class in middle school. I entered the classroom with a smile plastered on my face, armed with a bag of stickers and name plates. When I asked the students to write their names on the nameplates, the first student took the nameplate crumpled it up, threw it in the garbage can, and walked out the door.

I was floored. I felt totally unprepared for the experience. I was forced to write that student a discipline slip, which I really didn't want to do on my very first day as a substitute teacher. I thought it would make me look incompetent. I thought it would show that I did not know what I was doing. I felt like an imposter just playing teacher. But I adjusted to the situation at hand and did what I needed to do. In writing that student up, I set the tone for the day and showed that I meant business.

An Ounce of Prevention

As I continued to work as a substitute teacher, I developed some strategies to help me avoid writing students up or sending them to the office. I learned that, metaphorically speaking, an ounce of prevention is worth a pound of cure. In other words, if I set a positive tone with clear expectations when I first entered the classroom, I could prevent many negative behaviors from taking place. I tried to use positive techniques to encourage good behavior. The methods outlined in this book will start you off on the path to a meaningful and fulfilling career in substitute teaching.

Experience Is the Best Teacher

I survived that first day as a substitute teacher and I learned from it. And it truly did get easier over time. I learned that every classroom is very different, and that you need to adjust to meet your students' needs. I enjoyed visiting many classrooms and I learned so much by observing the different learning environments. I jotted down notes when I saw interesting ideas and later used many them in my own classroom. The experience that I gained as a substitute teacher was invaluable and it helped me to become a more successful teacher today.

Find Your Best Fit

I discovered that I truly loved working with the younger elementary school kids, a grade level that I would later go on to teach for many years. However, I found middle school to be particularly challenging, although many people love teaching at that grade level. Find which grade works well for you, and let your placement coordinator know where you are interested in teaching.

In the following chapters, I will share some pointers to help you embark on your career as a successful substitute teacher. From planning ahead to classroom management, this book will provide you with useful tips to make substitute teaching a positive and meaningful experience.

BE PREPARED

Preparation is key to successful student teaching. Being prepared will help pave the way for a smooth school day. Here are some pointers to keep in mind before you head for the classroom.

Dress the Part

Remember that you are a professional. If you want to make a good first impression on the principal, staff, and students, be sure to dress professional. Ditch the yoga pants, jeans, sneakers, and flip- flops. Instead opt for professional pants and tops. Women can also wear comfortable dresses and skirts, but remember you might be on the floor helping young students with games or learning center activities. Men should wear a nice shirt, slacks, and maybe a tie.

Fuel Up

Be sure to pack a snack and a lunch. Some schools may have vending machines or a cafeteria, others may not. It's best to be prepared by bringing something to eat for lunch. It's tough to make it through the school day when your tank is running on empty!

Pack Your Bag

You may want to invest in a tote bag or soft briefcase. Before you leave the house, be sure to have your bag stocked with any supplies that you may need that day. I suggest bringing the following items:

- extra pencils
- pens
- blank paper
- sticky notes
- Paper clips
- Red pen
- Highlighter

Student Work

You should also come prepared with work for the students in case there are no lessons plans for you.

Quick and easy time fillers include:

- seasonal word searches
- crossword puzzles
- coloring sheets
- Graphic organizers

- books to read aloud.

You may want to stop at a local copy shop, to make sure that you have at least one set of 30 worksheets in case there's no time to use the copy machine or in case it's broken. (A far too common occurrence in elementary schools!)

Map Your Trip

If possible, find where your school is located the night before you begin your teaching assignment. You can use the Internet to map the quickest route to your school. It might help to use GPS to find the most convenient route. I suggest driving to the school and seeing where you will park ahead of time, in order to avoid chaos and confusion during the morning commute.

I still remember one experience I had as a substitute teacher. I was called the night before to sub at a nearby school. I thought I had a pretty good idea where it was located, so I did not map it out beforehand. When I drove to the spot where I thought the school was located, I realized it was not there and it was nowhere in sight.

I drove around the neighborhood aimlessly and after making several panicked phone calls, I finally found the school. Unfortunately, I was already late. The school day had begun and the principal had to find another teacher to cover the morning activities. I hurried into the office, apologizing to the principal for being lost. I'm sure I didn't make a great first impression. And starting the morning flustered and frazzled set the tone for the rest of the day. After that experience, I always made certain to find out exactly where the school was before I left the house.

Get an Early Start

Set your alarm early so that you will have time to get ready and arrive at least 30 minutes before the students. This will give you time to become familiar with the building and review lesson plans before your day begins.

GET TO KNOW YOUR SCHOOL

By arriving early, you will give yourself time to get to know the building before the day begins and become familiar with your surroundings and the building procedures.

Check in at the Office

Enter through the main door and be sure to visit the office when you first arrive. Introduce yourself and let the receptionist know which assignment you were called for. You may need to sign in, get directions to your classroom, and get a visitors' ID badge before you head to your classroom. Bring your driver's license or another form of idea in case identification is needed. Safety is of utmost importance in many elementary schools and they are very careful about letting people into the building.

Finding Your Way around the Building

You may want to find the following places in the building in order to feel familiar with the school:

- The cafeteria
- The gym
- Student restrooms
- Teacher restrooms
- Teachers break room
- The exit
- Door to the playground

Helpful Colleagues

Don't be afraid to ask for help. Most teachers started out as a substitute teacher and they remember what it's like being in a new building. Most teachers are helpful and are willing to point you in the right direction.

Emergency Procedures

Safety is a foremost concern in many schools today. You may want to acquaint yourself with the school' s procedures for the following events:

- Fire drills
- Weather drills
- Active Shooter drills

- Emergency Evacuations

By getting to know the building and procedures, you'll feel more confident and you'll be ready to start a successful school day.

GET TO KNOW THE CLASSROOM

Even more important than getting to know the building, it is essential that you become familiar with the classroom where are you will be teaching. Again, arriving early morning will provide time to get acquainted with your surroundings and will help ensure that things run more smoothly throughout the school day.

Lesson Plans

Typically you will find a sub folder on the teacher's desk containing lesson plans, a seating chart, and the daily schedule. Be sure to review the lesson plans so that you know what activities you will be doing throughout the day. Gather any materials that you may be using during your lessons and have them ready for easy access during the day.

Post the Schedule

You may want to list the schedule on the board for both yourself and the students to view. You can have a student erase each activity as you complete it. This visual helps to keep students focused and on task. It also provides an easy reference for you as you complete your lessons throughout the day.

Teachers' Manuals

Usually, the teachers' manuals will be located on her desk. It's helpful to look ahead and find the pages that you will be using. I like to mark them with a sticky note. This helps you to quickly open to the pages you need during lessons. You can also jot notes on the sticky notes about things that you want to cover during class. You might want to stack the manuals in the order that you will be using them. The less down time you have between activities, the fewer opportunities for student misbehavior.

Computer

You may need to use the computer to record attendance. See if you are able to login and if not ask a nearby teacher for help.

Smartboard

Many classrooms are equipped with a Smartboard. Turn the Smartboard on before the students arrive and become familiar with its functions. Again, if you are having trouble don't be afraid to ask a nearby teacher for help. A reliable student may also be able to show you how to use the board.

Milk Money/ Lunch Tickets

Review procedures for collecting milk money or lunch money. Every school is different. In some classrooms you will not need to collect money or hand out tickets, but in other classrooms you might need to do this. If the teacher did not leave this information in her plans, ask the teacher next door.

Seating Chart

Keep the seating chart in a handy location so that you can use it while calling on students. Read the names ahead of time to begin to become familiar with the class.

Fire Drill

Look for a sign which indicates where the students will exit for a fire drill.

Classroom Aide

A classroom aide can be your biggest ally during the school day. If you are lucky enough to sub in a classroom with an aide, count your blessings! Be sure to ask for advice and help throughout the school day. Your aide will be familiar with the classroom procedures as well as with the students and their many different personalities. A classroom aide is an invaluable resource.

GET TO KNOW THE STUDENTS

It's important that you and your students get to know each other by name. Write your name on the board so that students will know who you are as soon as they arrive in the classroom. Meet students at the door with a smile as the enter. This initial encounter can help set the tone for a positive experience throughout the day.

About You

As soon as the students take their seats, introduce yourself. Tell them a little bit about yourself. Let them know that you're a real person. Tell how long you've been teaching or about your hobbies. Students will be eager to know about you and it will help you to make a more personal connection with them.

Names

Use your seating chart to call each name while taking roll. If you pronounce a name wrong, that's okay! Just ask the students to help you pronounce their names. And tell them to be patient with you and that it may take a few tries before you pronounce their names correctly. I teach in the school with a very ethnically diverse population and I always struggle to pronounce names correctly the in the beginning of the school year. Sometimes students giggle, but they are usually more than willing to help out with the names. It gives them a chance to be the teacher- a role they enjoy!

Name Plates

In many elementary school classrooms, students have nameplates on their desks. Use these name plates to call on students. Students will be more accountable when you call them by name. If the students do not have nameplates, you can give each student a sticky note or index card and have them make their own name plates. They can stick these on the front of their desks. They may want to color them and add a few designs for a personal touch.

The Name Game

You may also want to play the name game to get to know your students. You start the game by saying your name and something that you like to do. For example, I might say, "I am Miss Gilden and I like to read."

Then the first student repeats your name and favorite activity and they add their own name and activity. For example, student one would say, "You're Miss Gilden and you like to read. I am Bobby and I like to play soccer. " The next student would have to say the teachers name and activity, the first student's name and activity and then add their own name and activity.

Play continues until each student says their name and something that they like to do. It becomes a challenging memory game because the last student has to list the names of everyone else along with their favorite activities. During the game, you will quickly memorize the students' names as well.

I like to go last and say everybody's name and activity. I usually get stuck and need some help which elicits a lot of giggles from the students, but by the end of the game I can rattle off most of the students' names, which is helpful for the rest of the school day.

Clear Expectations
Before we begin the day, I like to clearly state the rules that I have for my classroom and what the consequences are if students choose not to follow the rules.

Often times they are the same list of classroom rules that the teacher has displayed. If they are already posted, you may just review these rules and tell students that you will be following the same system. If they are not displayed, you may need to post your own rules. My rules would typically include the following:

Raise your hand and wait to be called on.

Show respect.

Stay in your seat.

Keep your hands to yourself.

Try your best.

You may want to write your rules on chart paper and keep it in your bag so that you can hang them on the board as you travel to different classrooms. I also clearly explain what happens if someone breaks the rules. I will discuss consequences in the next chapter on Classroom Management.

By taking some time at the beginning of the day to get to know your students, it will help set the tone for a more positive experience throughout the day.

CLASSROOM MANAGEMENT

Good classroom management is the key to being an effective substitute teacher. This does not mean being a teacher who yells to maintain order. Instead, it means being a teacher who has good control over the class and maintains a positive attitude. Classroom management should start as soon as the students enter the classroom. As soon as they arrive, clearly spell out rules and expectations.

After reviewing your list of rules, let the students know about consequences both for breaking the rules and more importantly, rewards for following the rules.

Teacher's Behavior Plan

The teacher for whom you are subbing may already have a system in place for rules and consequences. If the behavior plan is listed in the lesson plans or posted in the classroom, I suggest you follow the teacher's system, since the students are already familiar with it. However, if the teacher does not have consequences clearly listed, you may want to use your own.

Name on the Board

One system that is easy and effective involves having students write their names on the board if they break a rule. This will serve as a warning to the students who break the rules and a reminder to other students that you mean business about classroom control.

If a student breaks a rule again, you put a checkmark after their name. When students have one or two check marks after their names, it is time to enforce with consequences.

Consequences

Possible consequences could include the following:

- Having the student write the classroom rules. (I only suggest this for grades three and up.)
- Having student complete a "Think Sheet" (see resources)
- A note to the teacher explaining the student's behavior.
- The student is not allowed to take part in a game.
- The student misses 5 minutes of recess.

- Being Sent to the Principal's office (I only use this as a last resort and try to handle discipline in the classroom whenever possible.)

Proximity

Simply moving closer to a student who is misbehaving is sometimes enough to redirect their behavior. Standing near a student's desk while continuing to teach can send the student a clear message without disrupting the lesson or calling attention to the negative behavior.

Calling on a Student

Calling a student by name is another way to redirect behavior with minimal disruption. If Tommy is talking to a friend instead of working on his Math sheet, you could say, "Tommy, what number are you on?" This may be enough to get Tommy refocused without escalating the situation.

Avoid Yelling

I try to avoid yelling at students or embarrassing them in front of their classmates. I believe that this is ineffective because it makes the students become defensive and often makes behavior worse. Some students will just tune you out when you are yelling constantly and other students will be frightened of you. It is not a good method to maintain classroom control.

Positive Reinforcement

I like to introduce a reward system for students. I believe that using positive reinforcement helps me to avoid using punishment and makes the day much more pleasant for the students and myself.

Recess as an Incentive

If the school allows it, you might offer a few extra minutes of recess at the end of the day as a reward.

Write the word RECESS on the board in big letters. Explain to the students that if they are listening well, the letters will remain on the board and they will receive some free time or play a game at the end of the day.

Explain to students if they are noisy or not obeying the classroom rules, you will erase a letter. If all the letters are gone by the end of the day, they won't be able to have the extra free time. You may also choose to add letters back to the board when students are listening. This visual reminder will help keep students focused.

Contest Between Groups or Rows

This is a technique that has been very effective for me throughout the years. I list student groups on the board according to how the students are seated, for example group 1, group 2, group 3, etc. I tell the students that I am on the lookout for good behavior. When it's time to take out a book or switch activities I say, "Let's see which group can get ready most quickly and quietly." The group with the best behavior receives a star next to their group name on the board. At the end of the day, the group with the most stars will receive a small prize. Most students are eager to earn that prize and will quickly learn to work together in order to win.

Sticky Note Rewards

You may also choose to distribute a sticky note to each student at the beginning of the day. Explain to students that you will be on the lookout for students who are listening well and that you will be adding stickers to their notes. Students who receive the most stickers will receive a small reward at the end of the day along with a note to show their teacher how well that they behaved.

Catch a Student Being Good

At time when the class is noisy or off task, instead of focusing on the children who are not listening, find a student who is behaving well and draw attention to him or her. For example, say, "I like the way Emma took out her book quietly and is ready to work." Immediately you will see other students doing the same thing in hopes of being recognized for their good behavior. Be lavish with your praise of good behavior and you may be able to avoid using negative consequences altogether.

Rewards

Rewards can include small items that you bring with you, such as pencils, stickers, or erasers. I like to keep a little treasure chest in my classroom and let the kids who behave the best pick a small prize at the end of the day.

Stocking up on prizes to be used on a daily basis can get expensive. Prizes don't need to be material things. Prizes can also include the following:

- A few minutes on the computer
- Sitting with a friend
- Reading with a buddy
- Being Line leaders
- Having name listed on the board as "Class Superstar"
- Being game leaders (in a game like 7-Up) *see chapter on Fun and Games
- Sending home a positive note
- Being selected as special helpers (paper passers, messengers, etc.)

By establishing a system of rewards for good student behavior, you will create a positive classroom environment and make for a pleasant school day.

ATTENTION SIGNALS

Before you can begin explaining rules or teaching a lesson, first you need to gain the students' attention. I like to use a quiet signal that draws students' attention quickly and quietly. The classroom teacher may already have a quiet signal that she uses, and in this case, I would continue to use it. If not, you may choose to use one of the quiet signals below.

The Attention Clap

Explain to students that you are going to do a special clap, and when they hear it, they are supposed to stop what they are doing and repeat the same clap back to you and then listen quietly for direction. Here's a clap sequence that teachers in my school often use:

Clap, clap (slow)

Clap, clap, clap (fast claps)

Then the students repeat it.

You can vary the pattern. It catches students' interest and they usually like trying to repeat the clapping sequence. Practice it a few times after you introduce yourself and then use it throughout the day as needed. Be sure to reward students who join in.

The Quiet Sign

You might choose to use a signal instead of a clap to gain students' attention. Some teachers raise their hand and hold up two fingers (like the peace sign.) As soon as students see the teacher do this, they stop what they are doing and make the quiet sign as well. Practice it a few times in the morning and students will catch on quickly.

One... Two... Three

Another technique some teachers use is saying the phrase, "One, two, three, all eyes on me." Students are to stop what they are doing, look at the teacher, and say, "Four, five, six, our eyes are fixed!"

Again, if the teacher for whom you are subbing has already established a quiet signal, I would follow her lead. You can ask a reliable student if there is a method they use when the teacher needs their attention. If not, I would choose one of these methods and stick to it, so that students don't get confused.

NO LESSON PLANS!
NOW WHAT?

Sometimes you may be called to sub in a classroom where there are no plans left for you. The teacher may have been dealing with an emergency situation and just did not get the chance to leave lesson plans. Or maybe you're subbing for a teacher who did not leave enough work to keep the class busy for the whole school day.

What can you do in these situations? Don't panic! There are some easy activities and lessons that can be integrated into almost any elementary school classroom. Here are some ideas that I found helpful when I was scrambling to find student work in classrooms without lesson plans.

Read Aloud
Bring a few books with you. A story can be read aloud as a reward at the end of the day. You can also read and discuss your book during

reading class. If you didn't bring a book with you, most teachers have a bookshelf or classroom library. Take a quick look and find a book that you think students will find interesting. When you're finished reading it, you can have the students take out their journals or notebooks to complete these extension activities:

- Write a new ending to the story.
- Tell about your favorite character and why they are your favorite.
- Tell about which character is most like you.
- Draw your favorite scene from story.

Buddy Reading

Ask a reliable student to tell you the name of the last story that they read in their reading text books. Read this story with the class, either calling on volunteers or reading in unison. When you are finished reading the story together, I would break students into pairs and have them read the story again with a buddy. This will help build their fluency and reading comprehension.

Spelling Bee

Ask a reliable student to give you their list of spelling words. Use these words to have a spelling bee.

Spelling Sentences or Story

Have the students use their list of spelling words to either write a story or write a sentence using each word.

Rainbow Writing

Have the students rainbow write their spelling words. Kids usually really enjoy this activity. Have them write each letter in a different color marker or crayon.

Word Race

Write the name of the month on the board. Tell students you will give them 10 minutes to see how many smaller words they can write using these same letters.

For example, from the word:

September

Students can make the words:

see, me, met, set, beet, seep, and many other words.

After a few minutes, see which student was able to form the most words.

Word Searches or Crossword Puzzles

Use some of the activities that brought you brought with you such as crossword puzzles and word searches.

FUN AND GAMES

A quick game is a great way to reward good behavior during the day. You might want to play a game before lunch break and again at the end of the day. Remind the class that in order to play the game they have to show that they are listening and working hard.

Here are some quick and easy games to play in the classroom:

Heads Up- 7 Up

This is one of my favorite games to play with my class. It's quick, easy, and most kids really enjoy playing it. It's also a game that requires quiet, so it helps to settle a class at the end of the day. I like to play it just before dismissal, when the kids have their coats and their bags already packed. It helps to maintain order at an otherwise hectic time.

Call seven volunteers to the front of the room. I like to choose seven students who have been behaving really well during the day as a reward. You say, "Heads down, thumbs up! "

The rest of the class puts their heads down on their desks, closes their eyes, and put their thumbs up. The seven volunteers quietly walk around the room and press someone's them down. Then they return back to the front of the room. When all of the seven volunteers have finished pushing down a thumb and have returned the front of the room, you say, "Heads up 7-Up!"

Then the students whose thumbs were pressed down guess which of the volunteers tapped their thumb. If they guess correctly, then they get to stand in front of the room to be a new volunteer and the other person sits back down. When everyone is finished guessing, the game begins again when you say, "Heads down -thumbs up!"

Hangman

This is another easy game that you can play in a short time. It also helps to quiet the glass down. I'm sure you're already familiar with the rules. Think of a word and write dashes for each letter on the board. Create the hangman on the board as well. Have volunteers raise their hands to guess letters. Tell the students you will only call on them if they are raising their hands quietly. The person who guesses the word correctly comes to the board to create a new word. Remind them to only call on friends who are raising their hands quietly.

Eye Spy

This is a quick and easy game for younger children. Start the game by looking around the classroom and saying, "I spy something with my itsy-bitsy eye that is..." say a color and have students guess what you are looking at. Again, remind them that you were only calling people who are raising their hands quietly. The person who guesses what you were spying gets to be the new spy. Now it is his turn to call on classmates. Again, remind students to only call on classmates who are raising their hands quietly.

Four Corners

This game can get a little noisy, so I would only recommend it for calm classes. Choose one student to be the guesser. The guesser puts his head down and closes his eyes. The rest of the class walks quickly and quietly towards one of the corners of the classroom. Label the corners as 1, 2, 3 and 4. After ten seconds the guesser calls one of the corner numbers. Anybody standing in that corner sits down.

The guesser will count to ten again as the students walk to a new corner. Then the guesser calls another corner number and more students sit down. The game continues until there is only one person left standing in a corner. That person is the winner.

Around the World

In this game students compete against each other are using flashcards to complete math facts. The student sitting in the first desk stands up and walks over to the person sitting behind them. You show both students a flash card and the first person to say the answer wins the round. The winner moves on to the next desk. The loser sits down. Again, you show them a flash card and the first person to answer correctly wins the round. That person moves on to the next desk. Play continues until somebody makes it through the whole class. The person who has won the most rounds is the winner.

Sparkle

This is a variation of a normal spelling bee. Students like it because they get to move around and sit on their desks. At the beginning of the game each student sits on top of his desk. You say a spelling word and the person in the first desk says the first letter of the word. The person in the next desk says the next letter of the word. Play continues until the students have spelled the whole word. After the last letter of the word has been spelled, the next student says "sparkle" and that student needs to sit back down in his chair. Then the teacher says another word and the next student says the first letter. If any students say the wrong letter they also sit down in their chairs. Play continues until there is only one student sitting on top of his desk. That student is the winner.

By taking the time to play a quick game with the class, you can maintain positive classroom climate and motivate students to keep working hard throughout the school day.

TAKE NOTE

Substitute teaching can be a great way to collect creative ideas to use in your own classroom. Visiting a new classroom each day will expose you to a variety of organizational techniques, behavior systems, and classroom decorations that you may choose to use one day. Writing these ideas down will help you to remember them and keep you organized.

Work Log

You might want to keep track of the dates that you work along with what schools that you are at and which teachers you are subbing for. This might come in useful at a later time when you're deciding which classrooms you would like to return to. It also might be useful if you are seeking full time employment as you have documentation of the hours that you have worked. *See the resource section for a sample log.

Idea Binder

When I was a substitute teacher, I kept a notebook of ideas that I gathered from the classrooms that I visited. I suggest separating a binder into different sections where you can easily file your ideas and find them when you're ready to use them. Some sections could include:

- Classroom decorations
- Bulletin Boards
- Classroom Organization (mailboxes, homework collection, etc.)
- Learning center ideas
- Behavior Systems
- Seating arrangements
- Interesting lessons
- Worksheets
- Pictures

Say Cheese

Use your phone to take pictures of interesting bulletin board displays, decorations, or other things you find useful. You can store these pictures in your binder and use them for inspiration in your own classroom.

One word of caution - do not take any photos of students or work with their first and last names listed on it. Parents need to grant permission before their children can be photographed. Many districts require that release forms be signed before photos can be taken. I would err on the side of caution and avoid taking photographs of any students or documents with their names on it.

Extra Copies

With the teachers' permission, you might want to include extra copies interesting worksheets in your binder. Rather than throwing away extra copies, keep one for future reference.

LEAVING ON A GOOD NOTE

At the end of the day, it's important to communicate clearly with the classroom teacher to let them know who you are and how your school day went.

A Detailed Report

Leave a note clearly stating any work that you have covered or were not able to complete. You should also inform the teacher about what students were absent. Finally, mention student behavior. I would try to stay positive and first let the teacher know what students were particularly helpful and well-behaved. Then I would mention the names of students who may have had trouble listening with a quick explanation of what happened. There is a sample report which you may wish to view in the resource section at the end of this book.

The Students' Work

Collect any work the students complete and keep it neatly organized on the teacher's desk. Use paper clips to keep assignments separated and you may want to label them with sticky notes. Try to correct worksheets if you get the chance, if you don't have time that's okay! There's not a lot of down time in an elementary school classroom. I would leave tests and quizzes to be graded by the teacher when she returns. She may have her own method and grading system for doing this.

About You

Finally, thank the teacher for having the opportunity to work with her class and if you wish to be called again to this classroom, let her know that you're available in the future. You may wish to leave an email address or business card so that the teacher can contact you about future vacancies. A good substitute teacher is in high demand and the teacher will appreciate knowing how to keep in touch.

You're on Your Way!

Best of luck to you as you embark on your career as a professional substitute teacher. Remember to go easy on yourself! You'll have both good days and bad days and you'll learn so much from each experience. Don't forget to ask for help when you need it. Choose which grade levels and classrooms are the best fit for you, and pursue future teaching assignments in these settings.

Whether this is your first step in becoming a full-time teacher or you choose substitute teaching because of the flexible schedule and convenient hours, you're sure to make an important impact on the students in your classes. Enjoy the experience!

RESOURCES

These samples are included in the following pages:

- Substitute Teaching Log
- A note to send home for good behavior
- Stop and Think about the Rules
- A report for the classroom teacher

DATE:	SCHOOL:	TEACHER	NOTES:

Super Star Report

Just a quick note to let you know that

_____

was a super star in class today!

Thanks for being such a good listener while I was here!

_____

Substitute Teacher

Stop and Think About the Rules!

Name: _____   Date:_____

What rule were you having trouble following?

_____

_____

_____

_____

What can you do differently to follow this rule?

_____

_____

_____

_____

The Sub Report

Substitute Teacher: _____ **Date:**_____

Absent Students:

_____

_____

Work We Finished:

_____

_____

_____

Work We Didn't Have Time to Complete:

_____

_____

Helpful Students:

_____

Notes about Our Day:

_____

_____

_____

_____